What's in Your Pocket?

Collecting Nature's Treasures

Heather L. Montgomery

Illustrated by **Maribel Lechuga**

ini **Charlesbridge**

Dedicated to all who find strange and wonderful things as we explore together—*H. L. M.*

To all curious people—*M. L.*

First paperback edition 2024
Text copyright © 2021 by Heather L. Montgomer
Illustrations copyright © 2021 by Maribel Lechug

Published by Charlesbridge
9 Galen Street
Watertown, MA 02472
(617) 926-0329
www.charlesbridge.com

Printed in China
(hc) 10 9 8 7 6 5
(pb) 10 9 8 7 6 5 4 3 2 1

Illustrations done in digital media
Display type set in Liam by Laura Worthington
Text type set in Grenadine by Mark van Bronkhorst
Color separations and printing by 1010 Printing
    International Limited in Huizhou, Guangdong, China
Production supervision by Jennifer Most Delaney
Designed by Jon Simeon

Library of Congress Cataloging-in-Publication Data
Names: Montgomery, Heather L., author. |
    Lechuga, Maribel, illustrator.
Title: What's in your pocket?: discovering treasures in nature /
    Heather L. Montgomery; illustrated by Maribel Lechuga.
Description: Watertown, MA: Charlesbridge Publishing, [2021] | Includes
    bibliographical references. | Audience: Ages 4–8 | Audience: Grades 2–3 |
    Summary: "A science educator honors children's curiosity and pockets full of
    'stuff' by introducing nine scientists who collected natural treasures when
    they were young. Collecting, sorting, and playing with shells, stones, and
    other objects taught these young people how to observe, classify, and
    discover."—Provided by publisher.
Identifiers: LCCN 2020028058 (print) | LCCN 2020028059 (ebook) |
    ISBN 9781623541224 (hardcover) | ISBN 9781623544973 (paperback) |
    ISBN 9781632898975 (ebook)
Subjects: LCSH: Life scientists—Biography—Juvenile literature. |
    Naturalists—Biography—Juvenile literature.
Classification: LCC QH26 .M65 2021 (print) | LCC QH26 (ebook) |
    DDC 508.092/2—dc23
LC record available at https://lccn.loc.gov/2020028058
LC ebook record available at https://lccn.loc.gov/2020028059

The author would like to thank Shirley Baxter (park ranger, Tuskegee Institute
National Historic Site), Diego Cisneros-Heredia (research professor, Universidad
San Francisco de Quito), Larry Davis (professor emeritus, College of Saint Benedict
and Saint John's University), Kay Etheridge (professor, Gettysburg College, and
Maria Merian scholar), Bonnie Lei (Head of Global Strategic Partnerships, AI for
Earth, Microsoft), Meg Lowman (Executive Director, TREE Foundation, and Director
of Global Initiatives, California Academy of Sciences), and Dale Peterson (author
of *Jane Goodall: The Woman Who Redefined Man* and friend of Jane Goodall)
for their invaluable advice and expertise.

When you explore the great outdoors
and find something strange and wonderful,
do you put it in your pocket?

Scientists collect specimens so they can
observe the details of natural artifacts.

George found a strange seedpod.
He put it in his pocket.
He forgot all about it, until . . .

Pop!

Seeds exploded all over the room.
After that, George had to empty out
his pockets on the porch.

Nobody knew that George would grow up to be the famous scientist George Washington Carver.

He helped farmers grow peanuts and other seeds in poor soil. He discovered almost three hundred new uses for the peanut, including soap, glue, fuel, and a new version of peanut butter.

Will found beautiful blue eggs high in a tree.
Needing his hands to climb back down,
he held the eggs in his mouth.

Oops!

Will crashed to the ground.
He swallowed the eggs!

Nobody knew Will would become the famous naturalist William Beebe.

As an adult, he set a world record by dropping half a mile down under the ocean waves in a steel ball called a bathysphere. Will was the first person to see glowing fish and other deep-sea animals alive in their natural habitats.

Valerie Jane found wiggly, squiggly worms.
She wanted to keep them close,
so she put them . . .

under her pillow!

Her mother persuaded her to put the worms back in the garden.

Nobody knew Valerie Jane would become the famous primatologist Jane Goodall.

As an adult, Jane slept in the rain forest with animals all around her. She studied chimpanzees, learned their ways, and watched them use tools—a discovery that changed how people thought about animals.

When you explore the great outdoors
and find strange and wonderful things,
do you put them in your pocket?
Do you add them to your collection?

As scientists sort, compare, and categorize specimens,
they learn to see patterns within their collections.

Charles collected lots and lots of things:
colorful rocks, empty shells, and living beetles.

"Charles!"

His sister convinced him that killing
so many creatures was wrong.
So Charles let the living beetles be.

Charles didn't know that he would keep collecting throughout his life.

When Charles Darwin grew up, he sailed across oceans to collect beetles and birds and other creatures. He noticed that animals well suited to a place survived and passed their traits to their young, while animals not well suited died off. Over time, this could lead to changes in a whole group of animals.

Meg found flowers and shells and lucky stones.
She put them in her pocket.

She climbed trees and collected leaves.
She sorted and labeled and stuffed everything
under her bed.

Eeek!

Meg wasn't the only one
who liked the collection.

Meg didn't know she would keep climbing trees as an adult.

She didn't know she would develop new methods for getting into trees safely using slingshots and hot-air balloons. Those methods helped Meg Lowman and other biologists discover an entire world of treasures in the treetops.

Diego collected snails and slugs and scorpions.
Sometimes they escaped in the house.
For his mum's birthday Diego gave her a gift . . .

una lagartija—a lizard!

She loved it!

Together they marveled at the lizard,
then returned it to the wild.

Diego didn't know he would become a herpetologist who studies lizards and frogs.

He never guessed that he would get to name a new type of frog after his mother! Diego Cisneros-Heredia has devoted his life to helping people connect to wildlife.

When you explore the great outdoors
and find strange and wonderful things,
do you put them in your pocket?
Do you add them to your collection?
Do you make amazing discoveries?

Young collectors make significant
discoveries, too. Trained to see details
and seek patterns, collectors of any age
can surprise us with their finds.

Mary found lots and lots of fossils.
Her whole family collected them.

When her brother spotted something
sticking out of a cliff,
Mary dug and dug until she discovered . . .

an entire skeleton!

Young Mary's discovery helped people
realize that animals can go extinct.

Mary Anning lived in a time before people knew much about fossils or extinction.

When she was just twelve years old, she discovered a skeleton that didn't match any living creature. Scientists named it ichthyosaur, meaning "fish lizard." Ichthyosaurs lived during the time of dinosaurs and died out millions of years ago.

Maria found caterpillars.
She collected them. She painted them.

Then Maria discovered that caterpillars are part of . . .

a science surprise!

Young Maria showed the world that caterpillars turn into butterflies.

Maria Sibylla Merian lived in a time when most people did not understand the life cycle of insects.

People thought adult insects grew out of mud, rotting meat, or old fruit. When she was thirteen, Maria started collecting caterpillars. She watched them closely and painted what she saw. Later Maria created books about the wonder of metamorphosis.

Bonnie found creatures in tide pools.
She filled her pockets with shells and sand from the sea.

As a teenager, Bonnie collected sea slugs. She borrowed slugs from other scientific collections. She looked closely at slugs everyone thought were the same.

Young Bonnie's observations led to . . .

the discovery of a brand-new creature!

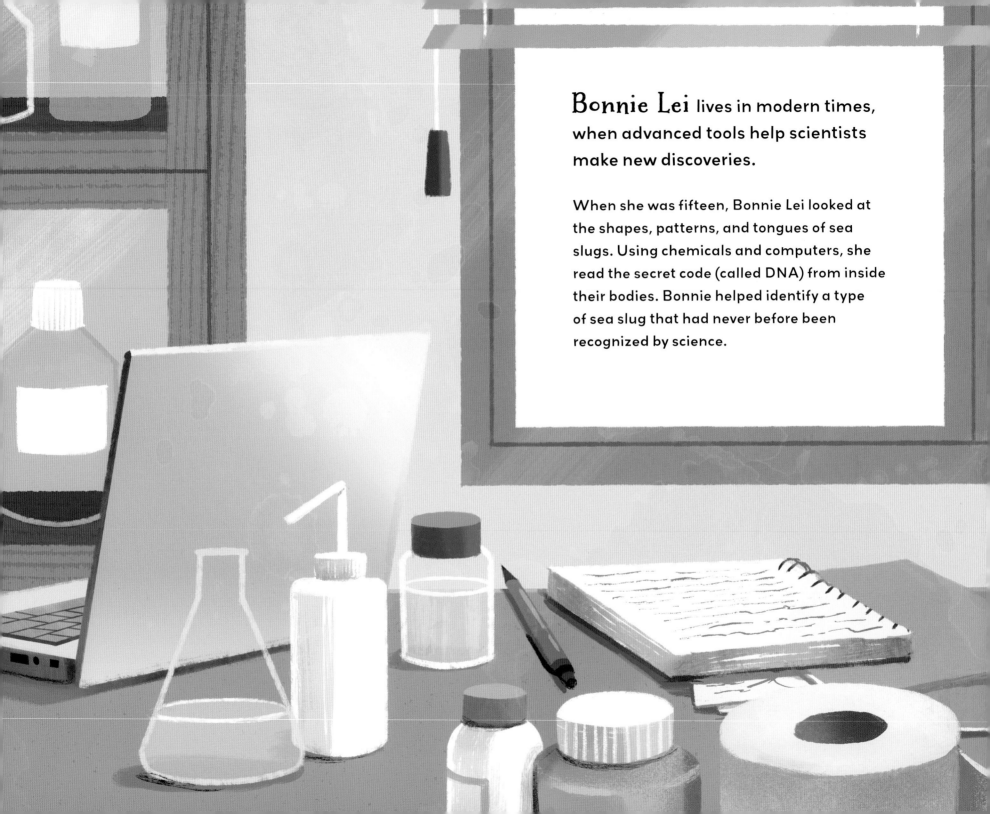

Bonnie Lei lives in modern times, when advanced tools help scientists make new discoveries.

When she was fifteen, Bonnie Lei looked at the shapes, patterns, and tongues of sea slugs. Using chemicals and computers, she read the secret code (called DNA) from inside their bodies. Bonnie helped identify a type of sea slug that had never before been recognized by science.

Throughout history, kids have found all kinds of strange and wonderful things.

They've created collections.
They've made discoveries.
They've changed the world of science.

Every discovery started with just one thing.
One little thing that could fit in a pocket.

What's in your pocket?

More About These (Grown-Up) Kids

George

George Washington Carver (1860s–1943)

George Washington Carver, a scientist and inventor, was born an enslaved person. After slavery ended, he was raised by his former owners, Moses and Susan Carver. Young George was often sick, so he worked inside, where Susan taught him to read. Outdoors, he collected wildflowers and grew them in a secret garden. He earned the nickname Plant Doctor by healing his neighbors' sick plants. As an adult, he taught farmers to sow peanuts, which put nutrients back into the soil as they grew. But people didn't know what to do with that crop, so the peanuts sat rotting in warehouses. That's why George developed so many new uses for the peanut. He is also known for his work with soybeans and sweet potatoes.

Learn more: *George Washington Carver* by Kitson Jazynka (National Geographic Children's Books, 2016)

Will

Charles William Beebe (1877–1962)

Young Will wouldn't stop until he found out everything about each bird, egg, or beetle he discovered. He went alone into the woods, snuck up on wild animals, and then carefully described his discoveries in letters to his father. Grown-up William plunged through rain forests, slid down mountains, and gazed into the ocean. No one knew what lived down there. No scientist knew how those creatures behaved. William wouldn't stop until he found out. He dropped into the ocean depths and set a world record by descending 3,028 feet (923 meters). William Beebe led a team of dedicated scientists to discover and describe more than eight hundred new species.

Learn more: *Into the Deep: The Life of Naturalist and Explorer William Beebe* by David Sheldon (Charlesbridge, 2009)

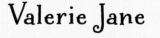

Valerie Jane

Jane Goodall (1934–present)

As a child, Valerie Jane had a menagerie of animal friends: worms, snails, caterpillars, a legless lizard, and a loving dog named Rusty. With her human friends, she created the Alligator Club and set up a museum, created nature quizzes, and raced snails. As an adult, Jane pioneered new methods for studying chimpanzees. She discovered that chimps kiss each other, that they make tools, and that females learn to be good mothers from their own mothers. Jane Goodall is the world's leading expert on these intelligent, expressive creatures. She inspires people around the world to protect chimps and all wildlife.

Learn more: *Jane Goodall* by Maria Isabel Sánchez Vegara (Frances Lincoln, 2018)

Charles

Charles Darwin (1809–1882)

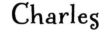

Charles never stopped loving science. As an adult, he took a five-year trip around the globe, collecting as he went. After the trip, he read, thought, and wrote about how species varied. Charles Darwin was not the first scientist to present ideas about the process now called evolution, but his theory of natural selection led to an understanding of how entire species might change. To create scientific collections, Charles did have to kill plants and animals. These specimens provided information that revolutionized scientific thinking.

Learn more: *One Beetle Too Many: The Extraordinary Adventures of Charles Darwin* by Kathryn Lasky (Candlewick, 2014)

More About These (Grown-Up) Kids (continued)

Meg
Margaret Lowman (1953–present)

Young Meg loved to collect and classify. When she grew up, she wondered what lived in the tops of trees. So in the Australian rain forest, she rigged, climbed, and dangled—and faced down thousands of stinging hairs in the gympie-gympie tree. To make things easier (and safer), Meg "CanopyMeg" Lowman built harnesses out of seat belts, created a tree slingshot, and designed hot-air balloons to study the treasure troves in treetops.

Learn more: *The Leaf Detective: How Margaret Lowman Uncovered Secrets in the Rainforest* by Heather Lang (Calkins Creeek, 2021)

Diego
Diego Cisneros-Heredia (1980–present)

Diego Cisneros-Heredia has discovered more than thirty new species, including a glass frog that has a belly so clear you can see right through to the stomach, blood vessels, and beating heart! To Diego, discovering and describing a new species is like giving a gift to humanity, connecting people back to nature. He has named animals after his mother, his grandmother, his mentor, and the authors of books he loved as a child.

Learn more: "Diego F. Cisneros-Heredia," www.cisneros-heredia.org (Diego's website, which is in Spanish, includes photos of Diego's work and interests.)

Mary

Mary Anning (1799–1847)

Mary Anning's father taught her to be a fossil hunter. She and her brother collected fossils and sold them to tourists. When Mary discovered the skeleton of a prehistoric marine reptile, scientists had to create a new name, *ichthyosaur*, for her unique find. Mary continued to find fossils throughout her life, discovering sharp-beaked pterodactyls and long-necked plesiosaurs. She also found bezoar stones and determined their true identity: fossilized poop!

Learn more: *Dinosaur Lady: The Daring Discoveries of Mary Anning, the First Paleontologist* by Linda Skeers (Sourcebooks, 2020)

Maria

Maria Sibylla Merian (1647–1717)

During the 1600s most people didn't understand where butterflies came from. Most artists didn't notice which plants insects lived on. Most scientists didn't study living specimens. Maria Merian did. She was able to illustrate the life cycles of nearly three hundred insects—and show which plants certain caterpillars lived on. Today we know that some caterpillars can survive on only one type of host plant. Thanks, Maria!

Learn more: *The Bug Girl: Maria Merian's Scientific Vision* by Sarah Glenn Marsh (Albert Whitman, 2019)

Bonnie

Bonnie Lei (1993–present)

Using the science skills she developed as a young person, Bonnie Lei is making a difference. From the tide pools in the land of her birth (the United States) to the coasts in the land of her ancestors (Myanmar), Bonnie is putting her deep-seated love of sea life to work. She uses science to answer questions. Are penguin nests getting hotter? Is that a problem? Which fishing gear is most harmful to sharks? Today she helps scientists across the globe use artificial intelligence and other technologies to conserve nature's treasures.

Learn more: "The Power of Penguins" by Bonnie Lei (*Harvard Gazette*, Feb. 22, 2013), https://news.harvard.edu/gazette/story/2013/02/the-power-of-penguins/

A Note from the Illustrator

There is something that unites scientists and illustrators: observation. It's the basic tool that helps both the child scientist and the child artist understand the world around them. I was a child artist, and I believe that there is no artist who doesn't love nature and its wonders. That's why I was excited to work on this beautiful project.

My creative process began with research. The search for documentation is the most entertaining part for me and where the first ideas begin to emerge. I collected dozens of photos about the time period and clothing of each character. I also spent a lot of time looking for information about the fauna and flora in several books about nature.

For the little treasure that the girl finds at the beginning of the book, I was inspired by a personal anecdote. Some time ago, my husband, who is a geologist, showed me a handful of small stones that he had found in a field, in an area that had been a shallow sea a long, long time ago. He told me that they were sea urchin fossils, about 90 million years old, from the Cretaceous Period. Wow! I thought that was so fantastic!

The sketching phase is the most complicated for me, so I need silence and maximum concentration. Once the sketches are finished and approved, the color comes out easily.

Now, with the job done and a smile on my lips, I can't help but think of all those little kids with pockets full of treasures who changed and will change the world.

A Note from the Author: My Collections

Visit my house, and you will see a basket of bones and stones beside my front door, a clutter of fossils on my windowsill, and a jumble of strange and wonderful things on my bedside table. As a kid, I stuffed my pockets full of nature's treasures. Later, when I studied biology, I realized that collecting, sorting, and playing with natural artifacts had taught me to observe, classify, and discover like a scientist. Still later, I learned that my habits were thanks to a type of thinking and learning called naturalistic intelligence. If you feel most comfortable outdoors, enjoy sorting items, or are passionate about nature, you may possess this kind of intelligence, too.

In the past, scientists took more from nature than we ever would today. Back then, there were fewer people and more plants and animals on the planet. Today, overcollecting can cause problems. Like modern scientists, I am respectful with my collecting. Many times I snap photos or draw pictures instead of taking an item from nature.

My Rules for Collecting

To respect nature:

* I collect only things that are not alive.
* I collect only if it won't hurt nature. I never take rare items or things an animal might need.
* I collect only if it is allowed. In the United States it is illegal to collect parts (feathers, feet, bones, beaks, even eggs) of many kinds of birds.

To respect the people I live with:

* I make sure my artifacts are clean and (mostly) stink-free.
* I have areas set aside for my treasures.
* I make sure my collections do not bother my family.

To respect myself:

* I don't put my hands where my eyes can't see (like under a rock or log).
* I learn about plants and animals that could hurt me, and avoid them.
* I never put unknown items in my mouth.

Field Guides

A field guide comes in handy when you want to label your collection.
Digital versions can be great for when you are out in the field.

BugGuide, www.bugguide.net
> A website where you can submit photos to identify insects.

*Flower Finder: A Guide to the Identification of Spring Wild Flowers and Flower Families East of the
Rockies and North of the Smokies, Exclusive of Trees and Shrubs* by May Theilgaard Watts
(Nature Study Guild Publishers, 1995)
> Part of a series of picture-based books on trees, ferns, berries, tracks, and more. Look for the guide
> for your region of the country.

Fossils: A Guide to Prehistoric Life by Frank H. T. Rhodes, Paul R. Shaffer, and Herbert S. Zim (St. Martin's
Press, 2001)

iNaturalist, www.inaturalist.org
> A website and app for cataloging photos of your discoveries.

Tree Key, http://eekwi.org/veg/treekey/index.htm
> A website that helps you identify a tree's species.

To download an activity kit including a discussion guide, journaling tips, and more,
visit **www.charlesbridge.com/products/whats-in-your-pocket.**

Selected Bibliography

For this book, I interviewed Margaret Lowman, Diego Cisneros-Heredia,
and Bonnie Lei. I also referred to many excellent books, journal articles,
and websites. These were some of the most helpful:

Darwin, Charles. *The Autobiography of Charles Darwin: 1809–1882.* New York: W. W. Norton &
Company, 1993.

Lowman, Margaret. *Life in the Treetops: Adventures of a Woman in Field Biology.* New Haven, CT:
Yale University Press, 2000.

McMurry, Linda O. *George Washington Carver: Scientist and Symbol.* New York: Oxford University
Press, 1981.

Peterson, Dale. *Jane Goodall: The Woman Who Redefined Man.* Boston: Houghton Mifflin, 2006.

Wilson, Leslie Owen. "The Eighth Intelligence—Naturalistic Intelligence." The Second Principle.
http://thesecondprinciple.com/optimal-learning/naturalistic-intelligence/.